HOW DO THEY DO THAT?

Contents

Behind the story	2
Rescue!	4
Saving lives	8
Life in space	10
Cleared for take-off	14
Match day	16
From beans to chocolate	20
Pizza restaurant	24
Making news	26
Getting heard	28
Quiz	30
Glossary	31
Index	32

Charlotte Coleman-Smith

OXFORD

Behind the story

We don't think much about the things that happen every day. We can watch TV at the touch of a button or order a pizza and have it in minutes. We scarcely glance up if a plane crosses the sky. Yet, if we look behind the scenes, a series of processes have taken place to bring us these experiences. Teams of **skilled** people have come together to make it happen.

On news programmes and on the Internet, we can see astronauts propelled into space. But what went on before the event to make it happen? (See pages 10–13.)

Most people only get to hear the end of the news story. But all stories have a beginning and a middle. This book takes you to places the public rarely see ...

What we see	What we don't see
	See pages 8–9.
	See pages 14–15.
	See pages 20–23.

Rescue!

DRAMATIC RESCUE AT SEA

A sailor fought for his life in freezing waters yesterday. The Search and Rescue team who pulled him out of the water almost certainly saved his life.

Sailor being winched to safety.

Search and Rescue teams are on stand-by 24 hours a day. If the call comes, they must be in the air within 15 minutes during daylight hours, and 45 minutes at other times. Every second counts.

The Crew

Captain: leads the operation
Co-pilot: takes control in an emergency
Radar/winch operator: locates the ship; lowers the winch
Winchman: performs the rescue

1. *'Mayday, Mayday, Mayday!'*
The coastguard picks up a message from a boat in distress. Using the radar screen, the coastguard locates the boat, then alerts the Search and Rescue team.

2. The crew put on their survival kit and run to the helicopter.

3 The helicopter takes off. As the crew fly over the sea, they see smoke coming from a flare. There's a man clinging to an overturned boat.

4 The winchman, who is attached to the winch and a stretcher, is lowered towards the sea. The winchman helps the sailor on to the stretcher. When the sailor is in position, the winchman gives a signal to the winch operator to lift them up.

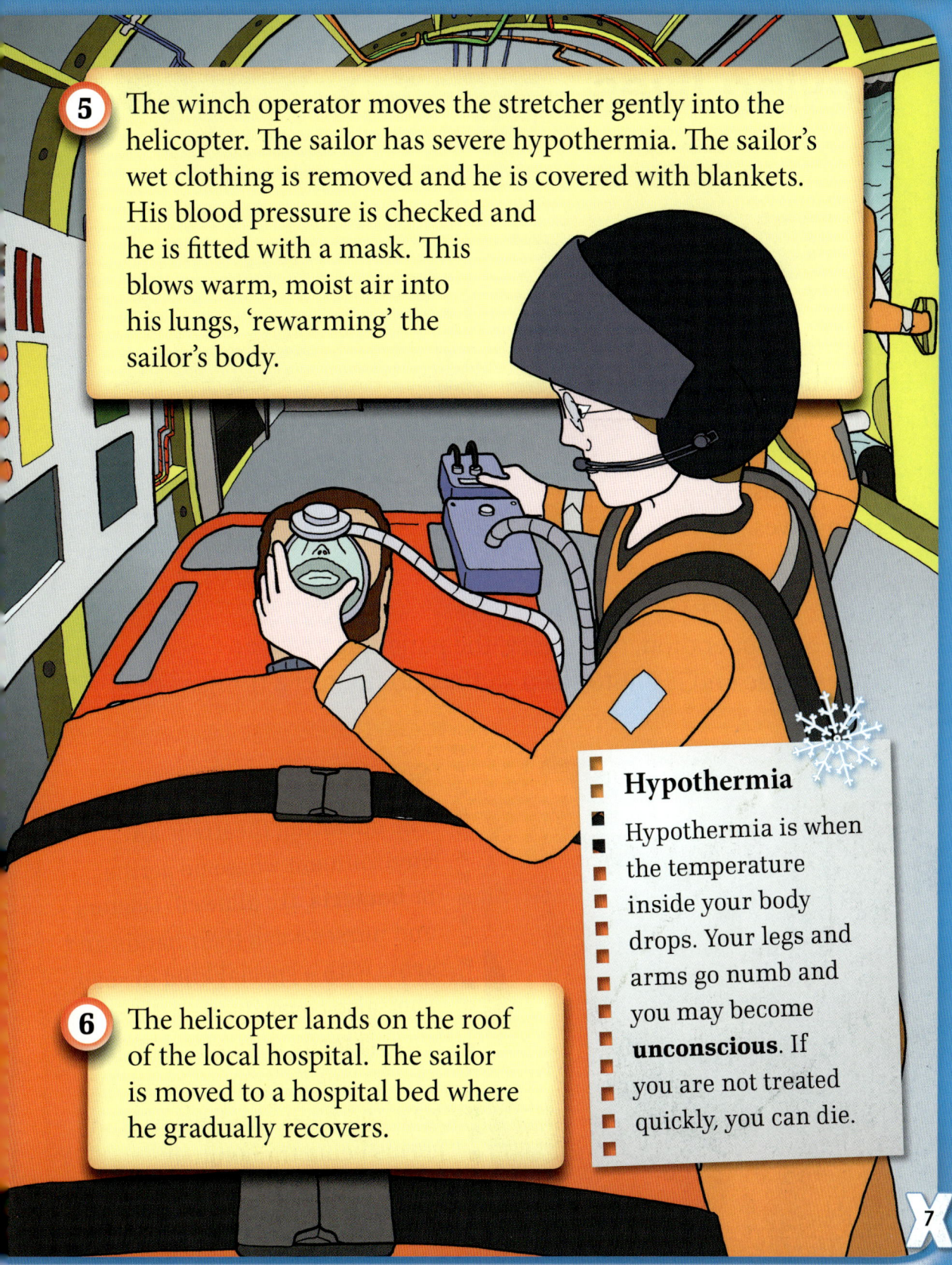

5 The winch operator moves the stretcher gently into the helicopter. The sailor has severe hypothermia. The sailor's wet clothing is removed and he is covered with blankets. His blood pressure is checked and he is fitted with a mask. This blows warm, moist air into his lungs, 'rewarming' the sailor's body.

6 The helicopter lands on the roof of the local hospital. The sailor is moved to a hospital bed where he gradually recovers.

Hypothermia

Hypothermia is when the temperature inside your body drops. Your legs and arms go numb and you may become **unconscious**. If you are not treated quickly, you can die.

Saving lives

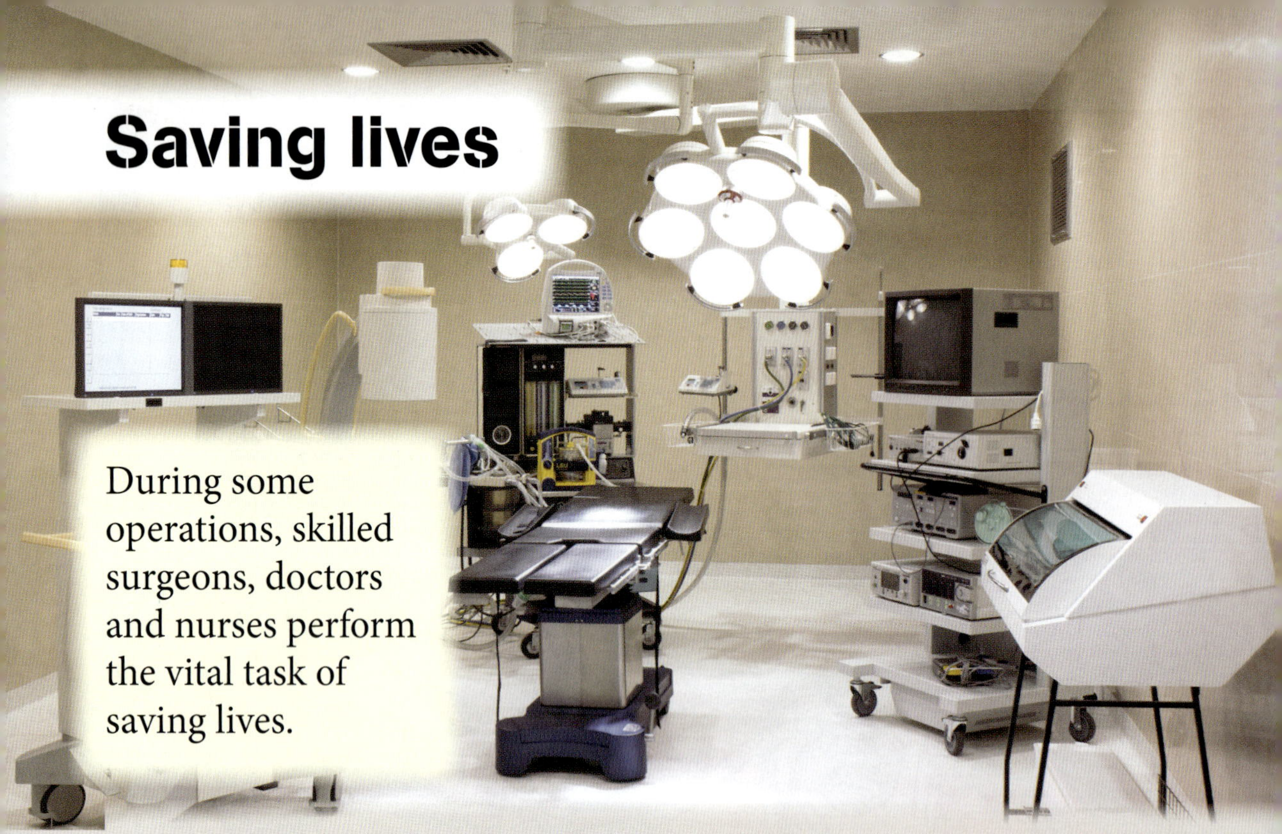

During some operations, skilled surgeons, doctors and nurses perform the vital task of saving lives.

Before the operation, or surgery, the patient is given an **anaesthetic** and is put to sleep so they do not feel a thing.

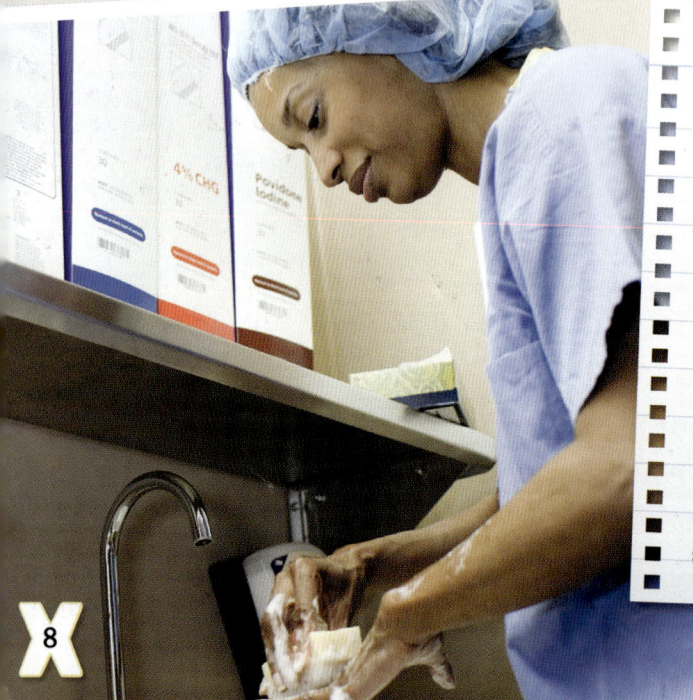

Squeaky clean

The operating theatre is an environment where no germs or **bacteria** are allowed. Doctors and nurses wash their hands and arms with a special kind of soap. They also cover their uniform with a **sterile** garment called a gown. Caps keep hair out of the way, and masks and gloves stop germs being transmitted.

Different types of life-saving surgery

Emergency surgery: this surgery is for serious cases that need immediate action. Operations are usually performed within 24 hours of the patient being admitted.

Keyhole surgery: instead of a large cut, the surgeon makes three or four small ones. A tiny telescope with a video camera is inserted into one cut. The surgeon watches the pictures taken with the video camera on a TV and controls the instruments **remotely**.

Organ transplant surgery: when a patient has a failing organ, e.g. a kidney, liver or heart, surgeons replace it with a healthy one donated by another human being.

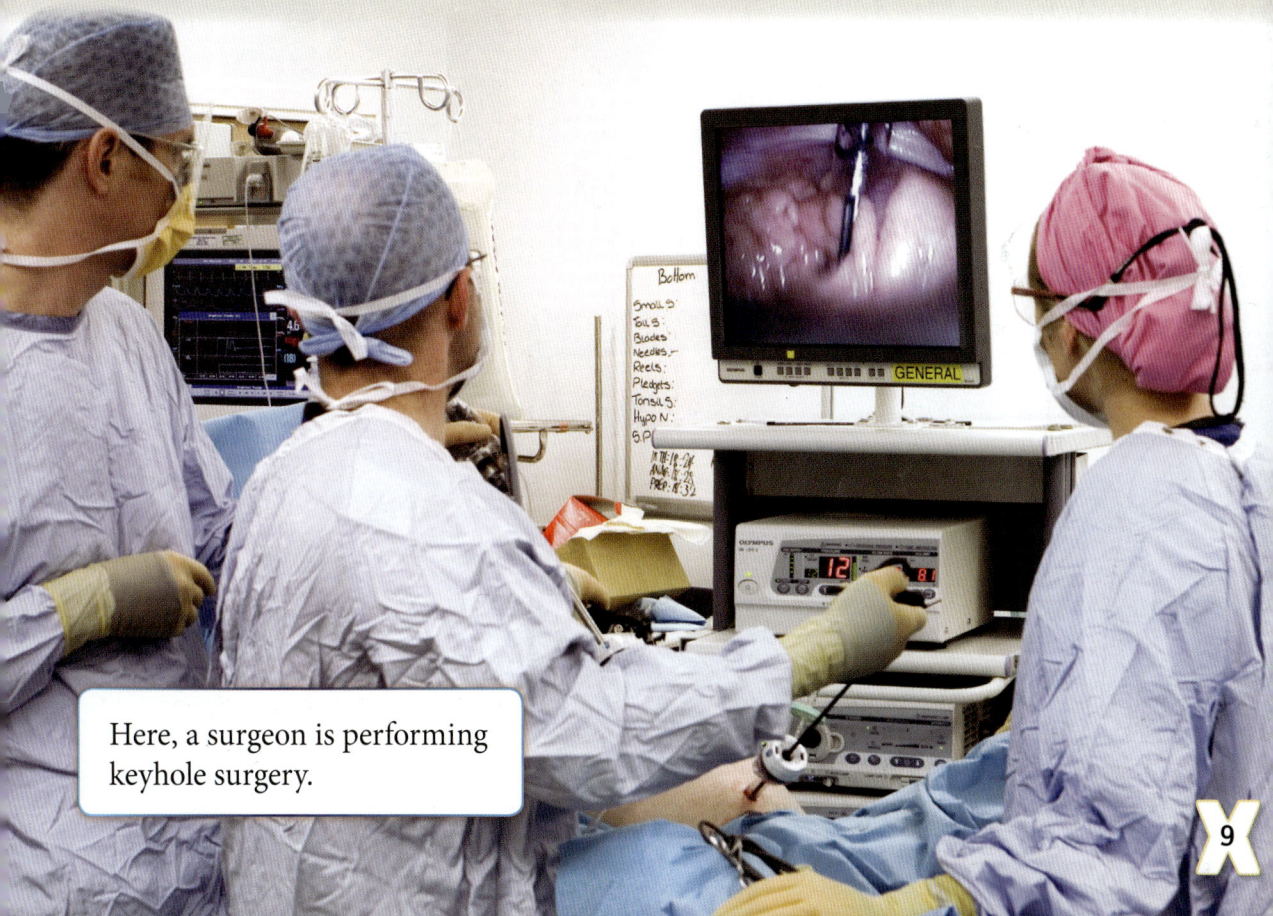

Here, a surgeon is performing keyhole surgery.

Life in space

Powerful rocket boosters fire into action, lifting 2 million kilograms of space shuttle into the air. Inside, there are seven astronauts heading for space.

Once in space, the astronauts will carry out experiments that will teach us more about Earth and the solar system.

Space school

Thousands apply to be astronauts every year. To make the grade you must:
- ✓ have perfect eyesight
- ✓ be super-fit
- ✓ be at least 163 centimetres tall.

Astronaut Soichi Noguchi tests out a new repair technique at the Johnson Space Centre in 2004.

Astronauts from the USA spend two years at **NASA**'s Johnson Space Center in Houston, Texas. Here, they learn how to adapt to life in space.

International Space Station

The International Space Station (ISS) is in space, **orbiting** around Earth. The space station allows astronauts to stay longer in space than if they were in a space shuttle. This means they can do experiments over long periods of time.

Frank DeWinne performing a plant growth experiment on the ISS in 2002.

Astronauts do not need to wear a spacesuit inside the space station. However, they are still affected by lack of gravity. Gravity is the force which pulls everything down and keeps us standing on Earth. When we drop something, it is gravity that makes it fall to the ground. In space, there is little gravity to hold the astronauts down. This means, for example, they have to sleep in sleeping bags attached to a surface, to avoid floating away.

When working outside the space station – making vital repairs or checks – astronauts need to wear a spacesuit. In space there is no oxygen, so an astronaut needs a spacesuit to help them breathe, otherwise they would be unconscious in 15 seconds. Temperatures are also extreme in space. Without a suit, they would fry or freeze depending on where the sun was. A rocket-powered backpack helps an astronaut to move around.

Tiny pieces of dust – micrometeoroids – can hit the astronaut at the speed of a bullet. A space suit protects an astronaut against these.

Cleared for take-off

When you get on an aeroplane, it's not just the pilot and flight crew who keep you safe. Air traffic controllers work behind the scenes to make sure the plane takes off and lands safely. They direct planes in and out of the airport and make sure there are no collisions or crashes.

The huge number of planes in the skies means that traffic jams can happen. Pilots listen to instructions from the air traffic control centre and wait for their turn to take off or land.

This air traffic control tower in Bangkok, Thailand is one of the tallest in the world. It is 132.2 metres off the ground.

Inside the tower

Inside the air traffic control tower, controllers use computers and radar to watch each plane. They may be in charge of several planes at once, so they must stay alert at all times.

An air traffic controller:
- helps pilots to fly around, rather than through, storms or bad weather
- holds planes in a 'stack' until a space comes up for them to land.

Very occasionally, accidents can happen. On 1st July 2002, a Russian airplane and a Boeing 757 collided above Überlingen, in German airspace. An air traffic controller had given wrong instructions to one of the planes.

Match day

When we see the world's greatest footballers scoring goals in front of huge, cheering crowds, it's easy to forget all the hard work that goes on behind the scenes.

High up in the stadium, TV and radio commentators get ready to broadcast the match.

In the police control centre, officers are watching what is happening in the stadium on **CCTV** cameras. More police patrol inside and outside the stadium.

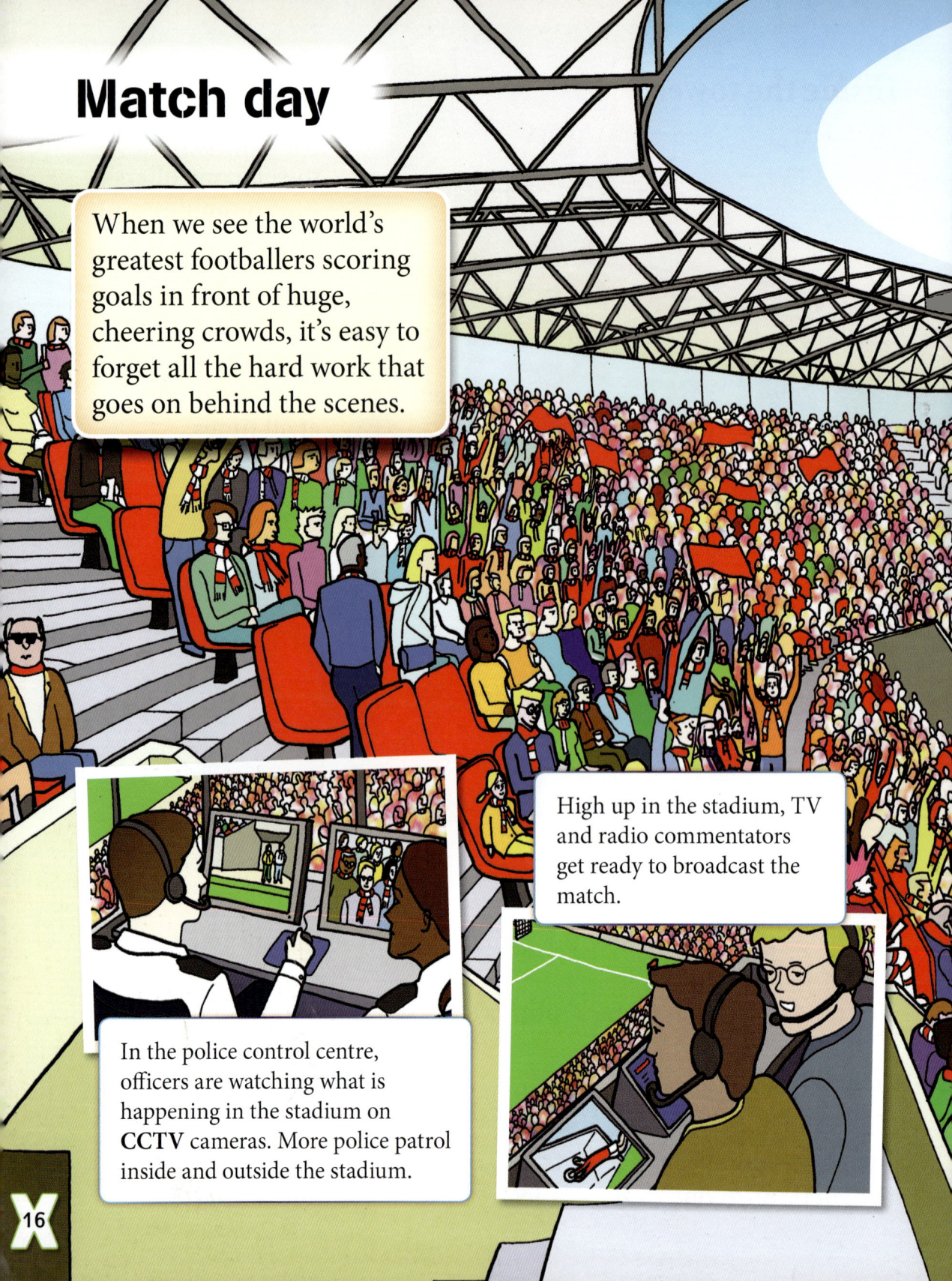

Kick off!

In the dressing rooms inside the stadium, players will put on their kit: team shirts, shorts, socks, shin pads and boots. The team that is playing in their own stadium is called the 'home team'. A visiting team is called the 'away team'.

Leading the players out on to the pitch is the referee and his assistants (dressed in black).

The training ground

As with all top sportsmen and women, the best footballers have to train hard to polish their skills. To prepare for their next match, the players meet at the club's training ground.

The coach will watch the players in training and think about who might be on the team for the next match.

Warming up

It's important for players to warm up properly so they don't pull or strain a muscle. After the warm-up, the players can practise their moves safely.

Here, members of the Paraguay national team stretch before a practice session.

Off the pitch

Injured players may receive treatment from the club's **physiotherapist**. The physiotherapist will help them get fit for action again.

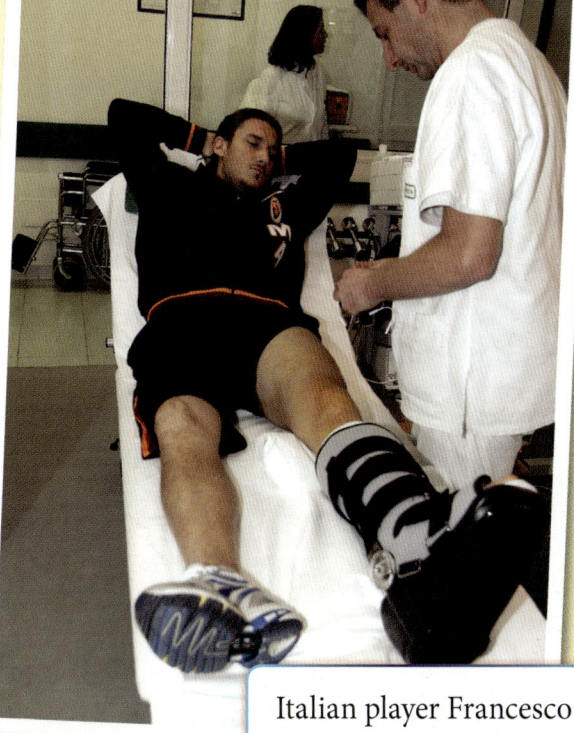

Italian player Francesco Totti receives treatment for a leg injury in 2006.

A coach talks to his team.

The coach will also talk to the players about **tactics** – how they can beat the other team when the next game comes.

Eat fit

Players must drink plenty of water and eat healthy, low-fat food that will help keep their bodies fit and well.

From beans to chocolate

Chocolate is a favourite treat for many people. But where does it come from and how is it made?

Bitter beans

Chocolate begins as cocoa seeds. The seeds grow inside large pods on cacao (*say* ka-ka-o) trees in tropical rainforests.

Fascinating fact!

Long ago in Central America, people called the **Aztecs** discovered that cocoa beans could be made into a bitter drink. The beans were considered to be so precious, the Aztec Emperor, Montezuma, kept millions of them in his storehouses.

Harvesting: the cacao pods are harvested using large knives. They are split open and the seeds and pulp are removed.

Fermentation: the seeds and pulp are left to **ferment** for five days. The seeds turn brown and become known as beans. They also lose some of their bitter flavour.

Drying: the beans are spread out and left to dry for up to a week. Workers turn them daily.

Shipping: the dried beans are packed into large sacks and shipped to chocolate factories around the world.

It takes 300–600 cocoa beans to make one kilogram of chocolate.

Inside the factory: from the beans to the butter

Once the cocoa beans arrive at the factory they are roasted at a very high temperature.

The shells are removed and the 'nibs' that remain are ground to a paste. The paste (also called cocoa mass) is pressed to separate the cocoa butter from it. Some of this cocoa butter will be used with the paste to make the chocolate.

A roasting machine.

Once the chocolate mixture has been made, a machine called a conche machine is used to make the chocolate smooth.

Final stages

To make chocolate bars, liquid chocolate is poured into moulds by machines.

To make chocolate with fillings, each centre is dipped in or squirted with liquid chocolate until it's evenly covered. This is called 'enrobing'.

Some chocolate is handmade by people called chocolatiers. This takes a lot of skill and practice. Handmade chocolates from Belgium, France and Switzerland are particularly famous.

Milk chocolate

1. Mix chocolate mass with sugar, milk, vanilla and cocoa butter.
2. Grind the mixture.
3. Put through a conche machine.
4. Temper (cool, reheat, cool) to create the perfect texture.
5. Eat!

Pizza restaurant

In the USA, about 350 slices of pizza are eaten per second. But what goes on in the kitchen of a pizza restaurant?

Show off!
Sometimes, you might see the chefs tossing the dough in the air to stretch it. This isn't really necessary, but it makes a great show!

Hot, hot, hot!
Pizza needs to be cooked fast and at a very high temperature – a scorching 650º Celsius.

Pizza dough

1. Make a circle of flour with a 'well' in the centre. Pour in warm water. Sprinkle in yeast. Leave for about 10 minutes for the yeast to become active.

2. Add oil and salt. Mix flour and liquid together to make a dough.

3. Knead well for 10 minutes.

4. Leave to rise in a warm place.

5. Knead the dough and leave to rise again.

Top that!

Favourite toppings from around the world:

India: pickled ginger, minced mutton and paneer (like cottage cheese)
Japan: eel, squid and Mayo Jaga (mayonnaise, potato, bacon)
Netherlands: double meat, double cheese, double onion ('Double Dutch')

Making news

When we watch news on TV, the news presenters always look calm and relaxed. Behind the scenes, however, teams of journalists and editors have been busy for hours getting every detail just right.

Gathering the news

Journalists in the newsroom need to check the facts of the news item. They make phone calls, check emails and write the scripts for the presenter to read out on TV.

Getting the pictures

TV needs pictures to help tell the story. The editor sends out camera crews to film what is happening. People also send in pictures, sometimes from their mobile phones.

At the scene, the reporter is filmed 'live' talking to the police and to people who saw the incident.

Putting it together

Back in the studio, the editing team uses equipment to combine pictures and sounds for the news report.

On air

The presenters read the script from a machine called an Autocue. An earpiece is fitted to allow the studio team to speak to the presenters.

Getting heard

When you listen to your favourite band on a CD or on an MP3 player you are hearing the end result of a lot of hard work.

The Arctic Monkeys live on stage.

Getting hooked

When a songwriter composes a new song, they try to include a 'catchy' part to hook the listener. This is often in the chorus.

After a band has written several songs, the members will try to get an agent to help record them.

Each song is recorded in stages. These are mixed together to create the finished sound you hear.

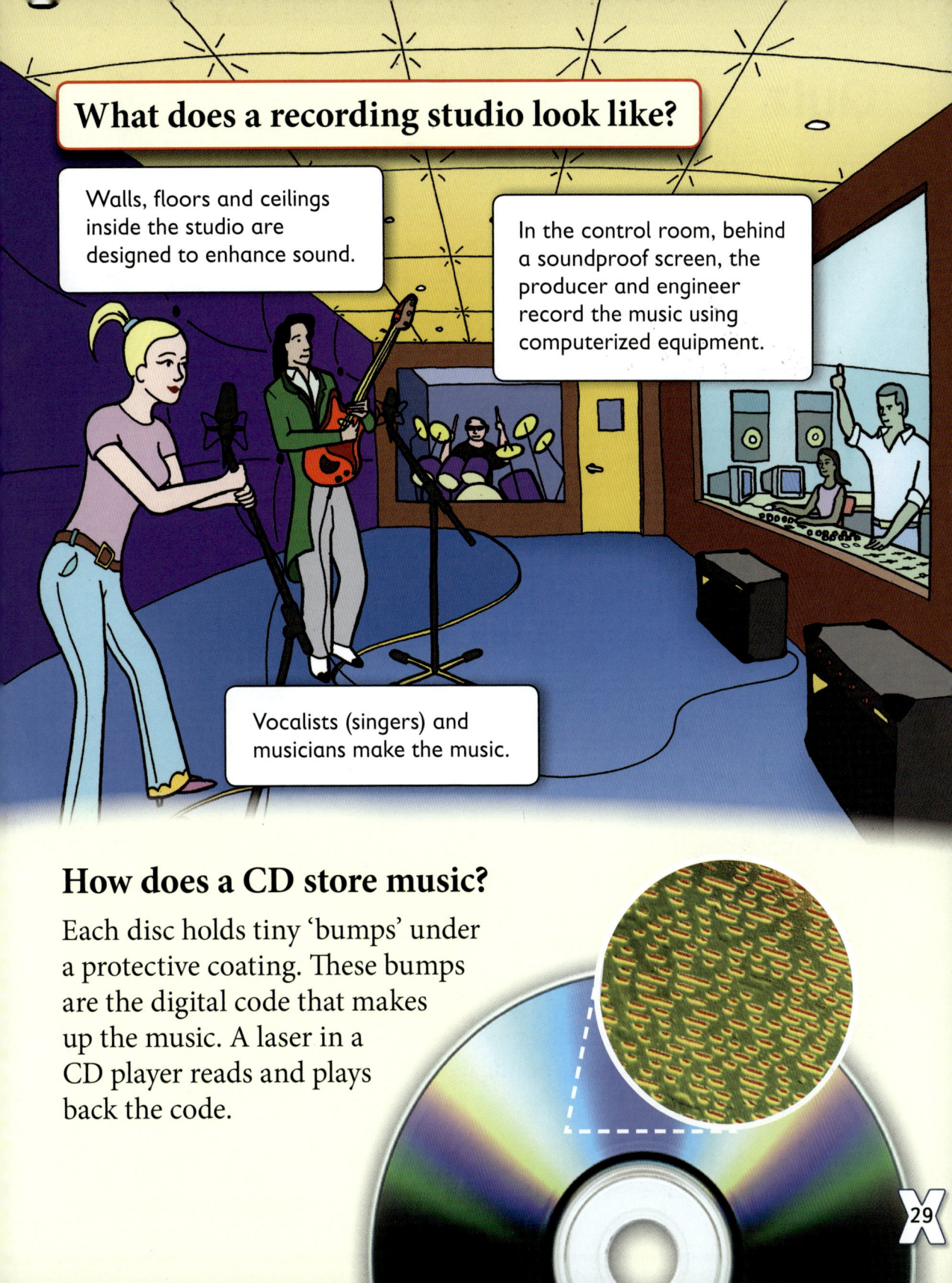

What does a recording studio look like?

Walls, floors and ceilings inside the studio are designed to enhance sound.

In the control room, behind a soundproof screen, the producer and engineer record the music using computerized equipment.

Vocalists (singers) and musicians make the music.

How does a CD store music?

Each disc holds tiny 'bumps' under a protective coating. These bumps are the digital code that makes up the music. A laser in a CD player reads and plays back the code.

Quiz

Can you remember what these people do behind the scenes?

1 A winchman
   a is the pilot of the Search and Rescue team.
   b lowers the winch from a helicopter.
   c performs the rescue using a winch.

2 During an operation, a keyhole surgeon
   a uses large tools.
   b tells the nurses how to use the tools.
   c uses microscopic tools.

3 An astronaut
   a writes about people who go into space.
   b is a pilot who never goes into space.
   c travels and carries out experiments in space.

4 An air traffic controller
   a flies the plane when the pilot is ill.
   b directs the pilot to take off and land.
   c helps planes to fly through storms.

5 A football coach
   a gives the players a massage before every match.
   b decides which players will play in a match.
   c drives the players to a match.

6 A TV journalist
   a researches and writes news reports.
   b films events which make up the news.
   c reads the news on TV.

Answers on page 32.

Glossary

anaesthetic	a substance or gas that makes you unable to feel pain
Aztecs	native people living in Mexico from the 14th to the 16th century
bacteria	tiny organisms, some of which can cause diseases
CCTV	stands for closed-circuit television
ferment	when a food or substance is broken down by bacteria and yeasts
NASA	stands for National Aeronautics and Space Administration – an agency of the US government
orbit	the path in space of something moving around the sun or a planet
physiotherapist	a person who uses massage and heat to treat disease and injury
remotely	from a distance and without any physical contact
skilled	having the ability to do something very well
sterile	completely clean and free from germs
tactic	the method used to achieve something
unconscious	in a very deep sleep

Index

air traffic controller	14–15, 30
astronaut	10–13, 30
bands	28
cocoa beans	20, 21, 22
football coach	18, 19
football stadium	16–17
International Space Station	12–13
Johnson Space Center	11
physiotherapist	19
pizza chef	24
police control centre	16
recording studio	29
Search and Rescue	4–7
surgery	8–9
training ground	18
TV journalist	26, 30
TV news presenter	26, 27
TV news reporter	27
TV newsroom	26
winchman	5, 6, 30

Answers to quiz

1c   2c   3c   4b   5b   6a